This

……………………………………

……………………………………

……………………………………

Christmas Stories

Stories for

5 to 7

year olds

Written by Hettie Bingham, Gaby Goldsack,
Sue Nicholson, Claire Noonan,
Kath Jewitt and Jan Astley

Illustrated by Leighton Noyes
(Graham-Cameron Illustration)

First published by Parragon in 2007

Parragon
Queen Street House
4 Queen Street
BATH BA1 1HE, UK

ISBN 978-1-4075-0166-6
Printed in England

Christmas Stories

Stories for

5 to 7

year olds

Parragon

Bath · New York · Singapore · Hong Kong · Cologne · Delhi · Melbourne

Contents

A Woodland Christmas

by Gaby Goldsack

One snowy Christmas Eve, in Greenacre Wood, Mr and Mrs Woodmouse were just hanging the twins' Christmas stockings in front of the fireplace when the roof above their burrow gave a worrying creak.

"I wonder what that is?" said Mr Woodmouse. "I'd better go outside and check that everything is okay."

Mr Woodmouse scurried away and scampered back a minute later, shouting and yelling at the top of his voice:

"Quickly, get out of here now! The roof is going to fall in!" He bundled Mrs Woodmouse out of the door. Then, without a thought for his own safety, he charged into the twins' bedroom and scooped them out of their bunkbeds.

"Is Father Christmas here?" asked Midge sleepily.

"Sorry, no," cried Mr Woodmouse, as he charged out of the house with a twin under each arm. He had just made it out, when there was an enormous CRASH behind him. He whirled round, just in time to see their beloved burrow disappearing beneath a mountain of snow.

"How awful!" cried Mrs Woodmouse. "Our beautiful home has gone."

"Along with everything in it. Even our clothes," wailed Mr Woodmouse, noticing that the twins, who were dressed in their nightclothes, were beginning to shiver.

"I'm c...c...cold," shivered Mo. "What are we going to do?" Mrs Woodmouse pulled the twins beneath her warm shawl and cuddled them close.

"Don't worry, we'll think of something," she reassured them.

"I know," said Mr Woodmouse. "Let's go to Grandma and Grandpa's house. They only live on the other side of the wood."

"But how will Father Christmas know where to bring our presents?" wailed Midge.

"Don't you worry about that," smiled Mrs Woodmouse. "He'll know where to find you. He's clever like that. But just in case, I'll pin a note to the tree by our old burrow, telling him where we've gone."

Mr and Mrs Woodmouse each hugged a young woodmouse to their side as they fought their way along a woodland path through the snow blizzard. It was very windy and the snow was falling hard so their progress was very slow indeed.

"Are we there yet?" asked Mo after they had been walking for some time.

"No," said Mrs Woodmouse.

"Well, where are we?" asked Midge.

Mr Woodmouse stopped and looked around. "Er, I don't know," he said slowly. "Something tells me we've been going round in circles. I'm sure we've been past that red door before."

"Ooooh! What was that?" cried Mrs Woodmouse, as something in the wood let out a loud groan.

The Woodmouse family huddled together and shook with fear. Then, much to their surprise, a door swung open in the roots of a nearby tree.

"Hello," cried a friendly voice. "What are you doing out there on this cold, snowy night? Quickly, come in before you freeze." Before the Woodmouse family knew what was happening, they found themselves in a cosy underground home, in front of a roaring log fire.

"I'm Mr Mole," said their new friend. "You must be the Woodmouse family. Why aren't you at home waiting for Father Christmas to come?"

After Mr Woodmouse had explained all about the disappearing house, Mr Mole invited them to stay until morning. Mrs Woodmouse was about to accept, when Midge interrupted.

"Oh, no," he cried. "We've got to go to Grandma and Grandpa's house because that's where we told Santa we'd be."

And so, after they'd warmed themselves, the Woodmouse family set off once more. As they struggled through the snow, they sang Christmas carols to cheer themselves up. They were just passing a hole in a tree, when a furry head popped out. It was Squirrel.

"What's all this?" called Squirrel. "Surely you shouldn't be out on such a snowy Christmas Eve?"

"No," replied Mrs Woodmouse, trying very hard not to shiver. "Our burrow has been buried by snow and we're on our way to my parents' home for Christmas."

"Well, don't just stand there shivering," cried Squirrel. "Come in for a while."

The Woodmouse family were only too happy to stop for a rest. It was a tiring business trudging through the snow. And they were even happier when Squirrel gave them some of his delicious hazelnuts to nibble on. But they didn't stop long because they

didn't want to miss a visit from Father Christmas. They struggled on and on through the snow, which grew thicker until the path through the wood disappeared and they became quite lost again. Soon the twins' toes were so cold that they couldn't walk a step further and Mr and Mrs Woodmouse had to carry them. Poor Mrs Woodmouse was so tired that she kept stumbling. Then, just as she thought she could go no further, she heard the sweet sound of carol singers. The cheerful tune helped them all carry on until they reached a clearing full of carol singers gathered around a glowing bonfire.

As soon as the carol singers caught sight of the exhausted Woodmouse family, they rushed over to help them. Mrs Rabbit, who was in charge, took one look at them and swept them into her nearby burrow. Before they knew what was happening, they found themselves bundled into warm clothes and sipping on sweet hot chocolate. "It's no night to be out and about dressed in next to nothing," she tutted. "Tiny woodmice like you should be tucked up at home on a night like this."

Mrs Woodmouse quickly told her that they were trying to find their way to her parents' house. As Mrs Rabbit listened carefully, she began to nod her head with excitement. "You must mean the old Woodmouse couple, who live beneath the Giant Fir Tree," she cried. "I know them. They don't live far from here at all. I can show you the way, and you won't even have to walk. Hop on my back and I'll carry you there now."

And so it was that the Woodmouse family arrived at the Giant Fir Tree in style. Grandma and Grandpa Woodmouse were very surprised that their family had come visiting so late on Christmas Eve. When they heard what had happened, they hugged Mrs Rabbit and thanked her for saving the day.

"You're welcome," smiled Mrs Rabbit. "But it doesn't sound like I was the only one who gave a helping hand."

"Yes," agreed Mr Woodmouse. "We were helped by lots of kind friends along the way."

Mrs Woodmouse explained how Mole and Squirrel had also helped them and Grandma and Grandpa shook their tiny heads in amazement.

"I've got a great idea," said Grandpa. "Why don't we invite them all over to a special Christmas party tomorrow, as a thank you for their kindness? There's plenty of room in this big old house of ours for everyone and we've got piles of food. We can get our friend Owl to fly around the wood in the morning to let everyone know."

Mr and Mrs Woodmouse agreed that it would be a lovely idea. "What do you two think?" asked Mrs Woodmouse, turning to the twins. But they were already fast asleep on the sofa.

"Well, I think it's about time we got to sleep, as well," yawned Mrs Rabbit. "Goodnight, everyone."

The following morning, Mo and Midge

awoke to find two Christmas stockings stuffed with presents at the end of the sofa.

"Hooray," cried Mo. "Father Christmas found us."

And after that, the day just got better and better. Grandma and Grandpa said that they could all live together in the big house under the Giant Fir Tree. Then, in the afternoon, all their new helpful friends arrived for a Christmas party to remember. There was singing and dancing and food galore, and nobody minded if it was snowy or not. They all said it was the best Christmas 'thank you' they had ever had!

Stowaway!

by Sue Nicholson

It was the morning before Christmas Eve. The toy-making elves in Santa's workshop had been up all night, finishing the Christmas gifts. Now every single present had been made, wrapped up, labelled and safely stowed in Santa's sack.

As they walked home for breakfast, carrying their little toy-making toolboxes, all the toy-making elves were chattering about the Elves' Christmas Party, which always took place on Christmas Eve while Santa went off to deliver the presents.

"I'm going to wear my gold slippers and new red party dress," Ellie was saying with excitement. "You know, the one with the green ribbons. What are you going to wear,

Ed?" she asked, turning to her friend.

"Oh, I don't know," sighed Ed.

"What's the matter?" asked Ellie. "Aren't you looking forward to the party?"

"I am," replied Ed. "But..."

"I know what it is," interrupted Ellie, "you still want to ride on Santa's sleigh, don't you?"

"Yes," replied Ed miserably. "I can't help it. I'd love to feel what it's like to whizz through the air and maybe I could help Santa in some way..."

"Well, he's never needed help from us before," said Ellie matter-of-factly. "Come on, Ed, we're toy-making elves. We make the toys. Santa is Santa, and he delivers the presents. That's just the way it is. And anyway, you promised to dance with me at the party!"

"I know, Ellie," said Ed. "And I do want to dance with you. I really do. It's just that I'd like to ride in Santa's sleigh, too!"

As they were talking, the two elves had wandered alongside Santa's sleigh, which was brimming with present sacks.

"You know, Ed," said Ellie, thoughtfully. "If Santa didn't know you were on his sleigh, then you wouldn't get into trouble, would you? Go on, Ed," she said excitedly. "Climb in the sack! Now, while no-one's looking! Santa is usually back before the end of the party to give the elves their Christmas gifts, so you'll get your sleigh ride and I'll get my dance – and maybe you'll stop looking so miserable," she laughed, giving him a playful push.

"Oh, Ellie! Should I really stow away on Santa's sleigh?" asked Ed, his eyes shining.

"Why not!" replied Ellie. "I won't breathe a word!"

"All right. I'll do it!" exclaimed Ed. "But

what about my toy-making toolbox?"

"Take it with you," suggested Ellie. "Quick, go on! Now, while no one's looking!"

Ed scrambled into Santa's sleigh, among the sacks.

"Have fun!" called Ellie. "Tell me all about it when you get back!"

"I will! I promise!" cried Ed. It was going to be a long wait until Santa set off, so he settled down between two soft sacks, made himself comfortable, and in no time at all he was fast sleep.

Several hours later, Ed woke up to the sound of jingling bells. The sleigh was moving! He climbed to the edge and peered out. Cold air rushed past his face, and he could see the twinkling lights of towns and villages far, far below.

"So you're awake then," called a cheerful voice. It was Santa!

Ed jumped, then blushed to the tips of his pointed ears. "How... how did you know I was here," he stammered. "I'm sorry, Santa," he continued in a rush. "I just...I just wanted to ride in your sleigh."

"I know," said Santa, laughing. "It's all right. In fact, you're the first toy-making elf who's ever wanted a sleigh ride and, to be honest, it's rather nice to have a bit of company."

"Really?" asked Ed.

"Really," replied Santa. "Come on, make yourself useful. Grab that present – the big one wrapped in red and gold."

All through the night, Ed worked hard, finding the right gifts in the sack and passing them to Santa, and holding tightly onto the reindeer's reins so they didn't fly off as Santa climbed up and down the chimneys.

"You've been a big help, Ed," said

Santa, towards the end of the night. "Now let's see," he continued. "We need a present for a little boy called James who lives at Fisherman's Cottage in the next village. Then we've got to deliver a doll to a girl called Natasha, and last of all, we need two presents for the twins who live at Elm Tree Farm."

"But I thought we'd finished," cried Ed.

"No, just three more houses," replied Santa, cheerfully, "then we must hurry back to the elves' party. Ellie will be waiting for her dance!"

"But we must have finished," repeated Ed. "I mean, there's nothing left in the toy sacks!"

"That can't be right," said Santa, looking worried. "There are always enough gifts!"

Ed scrambled down into the bottom of each sack to check, but sure enough, they were all empty.

"Oh dear. What can have happened?" Santa exclaimed. "Some letters must have somehow gone missing on the way from this village to my home at the North Pole. But I can't leave any children without Christmas presents, and now there's no time to fly back to the workshop and then fly back before morning. What shall we do?

What a disaster!"

"Don't worry, Santa," cried Ed. "You've forgotten – I'm a toy-making elf! Take me to the first house and I'll make a toy for James, as quickly as I can."

"Well, alright, if you think you can do it..." Santa agreed, obviously not at all sure that Ed could deliver on his promise.

Santa needn't have worried, though. Outside Fisherman's Cottage, Ed found some old cans of paint, a few pieces of wood, some rope and some scraps of cloth. He got to work with his toy-making tools and in no time at all, he had made James a beautiful wooden sailing boat painted blue and white, with three tiny wooden sailors that looked just like James and his mum and dad.

"Perfect!" Santa declared. "That's the best boat I've ever seen!"

At the next house, Ed made Natasha

a pretty doll wearing golden slippers and a red dress with green ribbons

"Just like Ellie," smiled Santa. "Natasha will love it!"

"We've only got time to make one more present," said Santa, as they got to Elm Tree Farm.

"That's all right," said Ed, as he got to work. "I know just the thing – something the twins can share!"

Soon there was a wonderful gift ready for the twins on Christmas morning – a shining rocking horse with a beautiful red saddle, a chestnut brown mane and jingling sleigh bells on its bridle.

"Well done, Ed!" said Santa admiringly. "What a beautiful horse. They'll be thrilled!"

Dawn was breaking when Santa and Ed climbed back in the sleigh and set off home at last.

"I've been thinking," said Santa. "How would you like to ride on my sleigh with me next Christmas Eve – just in case we're a present or two short?"

"Really?" asked Ed.

"Really," replied Santa. "Only don't forget to bring your tool-box."

"That would be wonderful," cried Ed. "Thank you Santa!"

Ellie was delighted when Ed was back in time to dance with her, and very pleased for Ed when she found out that he was going to be Santa's Christmas Eve helper. And on Christmas morning, four happy children were especially delighted with their beautiful Christmas gifts, made by Santa's stowaway elf.

Ed wasn't quite finished with toy-making that Christmas. The next day he popped into the empty workshop and made two more special gifts. He made a tiny sleigh for Santa, with every reindeer beautifully painted, as a 'thank you' for taking him on the ride of his life. Then he made a little music box with a dancing doll inside it, just for Ellie, for being a good Christmas friend.

Silly Santa

by Gaby Goldsack

Christmas was coming and Jayne and Sally were having a wonderful time. Every morning, while Mum was at work, the two girls would go to Gran's house to make Christmas decorations and other festive treats. Then, in the afternoon, Gran would take them down to the shopping mall to meet Mum from work. Mum worked in a store in the middle of the shopping mall, right next to the Christmas Grotto, where a jolly pretend Santa handed out gifts to passing girls and boys. Every time the Santa saw Jayne and Sally, he would wave and shout:

"Yo-ho-ho! How are you today?"

Then he would hand them a chocolate

or something else nice. After a few days, Jayne and Sally began stopping for a chat. They liked to admire the Santa's bushy white beard and wibbly-wobbly belly.

"You look just like the real Santa," said Sally one day.

"Even your tummy looks real," added Jayne.

The pretend Santa laughed.

"Well, that's because it is real, and I am the real Santa," he declared.

"Oh, no you're not," laughed Jayne. "We know that the real Santa's far too busy to work here."

"Yes," agreed Sally. "Gran told us that you and all the other Santas we see around town are pretend Santas, who are helping the real Santa because he's far too busy to be out and about at this time of the year."

"That's right," said Jayne. "The real Santa's at home getting ready to bring us our presents on Christmas Eve. And this year he's going to bring us Secret Detective kits! Well, we hope so!"

"I still say that I'm the real thing," laughed the pretend Santa, with a twinkle in his eye. Then he told them a joke that made them laugh so much that their own tummies hurt.

"Don't be a silly Santa," laughed Jayne. And that's when they decided to call him Silly Santa.

On Christmas Eve, Jayne and Sally rushed down to the shopping mall with Gran. She had some last-minute things to buy, and the girls wanted to go there to wish their new friend Silly Santa a Merry Christmas. But when they got to the grotto, they were surprised to find a new skinny pretend Santa, with a terrible fake beard, sitting in Silly Santa's usual seat.

"What do you want?" growled the

skinny Santa crossly. For you see, unlike Silly Santa, he didn't really like children all that much, and was fed up with his new job already. Children had been pulling his beard and saying he wasn't fat enough and jolly enough to be a good Santa.

"We're looking for our friend, Silly Santa. He's normally here. What have you done with him?" Jenny demanded.

The skinny Santa flicked his eyes to the left and the right and looked a little uncomfortable.

"No idea who you're talking about," he grunted. "Now scram before I get cross."

"I think he's lying," whispered Sally. "Something must have happened to Silly Santa. He wouldn't have gone without saying goodbye to us."

"Let's ask the lady in the sweet shop over there. She might know where he is," Jayne suggested.

"It was the strangest thing," said the sweet shop lady. "A gang of tiny men, all dressed in identical green suits, came and took him away. They seemed in an awful hurry."

"Poor Silly Santa! Somebody's kidnapped him!" Jayne gasped.

"We've got to find him," declared Sally.

Jayne and Sally went on and on at Gran, until she agreed to go around the shopping mall with them, on the lookout for anyone acting suspiciously. She didn't think for a moment that Silly Santa was in trouble, but she knew the girls loved to play at being detectives and didn't mind them playing their game for a few minutes. She had no idea that the girls were deadly serious and they had convinced themselves that Silly Santa needed rescuing. A surprised Gran was soon to find out just how serious they were!

"Look over there," cried Jayne. "That man's dragging Silly Santa into his van." Jayne and Sally raced across to the van.

"LET HIM GO!" yelled Sally and Jayne at the tops of their voices.

"A-hem," coughed Gran. "I'm terribly sorry, young man. These girls have made a mistake. That's not Silly Santa. It's a Christmas decoration." Gran was quite right. The man had bought a big model

Santa and was taking it home.

Sally and Jayne both felt a little bit embarrassed but they weren't put off. They were still determined to track down Silly Santa. They prowled around the shopping mall, with Gran in tow, until they arrived at some Christmas market stalls.

"What about him?" asked Sally, pointing to a man wearing a hat pulled down over his eyes.

"Yes, he does look dodgy," agreed Jayne. "He's definitely snooping around."

They followed the man around until he stopped at a Christmas decoration stall and pulled a notebook from his pocket.

"What's he up to?" whispered Sally, and they crept closer so they could listen.

"Can I see your market licence?" the man asked the stallholder. Jayne and Sally looked at each other and shook their heads. He wasn't a Santa-napper, after all.

He was just the market inspector.

Gran sighed.

"We need to go home soon. You can have five more minutes being detectives," she said.

Just then they heard a lot of noise and saw a crowd gathered around the enormous Christmas tree in the middle of the shopping centre. They definitely sounded like they were up to no good.

"Let's go," shouted Jayne, and the two girls charged off before Gran could stop them. They pushed their way through the crowd and saw a big sack beneath the Christmas tree … a sack just about big enough to hold a Silly Santa! Then Sally and Jayne dived on the sack and began to untie the ribbon holding it closed.

"Hey, what are you doing?" cried an angry lady.

"They're stealing our pressies," wailed

some children.

"STOP!" cried Gran. "These aren't Santa-nappers. They're carol singers. And that sack's full of presents, not Silly Santa. I really think you'd better stop playing detectives now before you get into any more trouble."

Sally and Jayne said sorry to the rather cross carol singers and left the shopping mall, feeling sad and puzzled about the missing Silly Santa.

"Don't worry," said Dad at bedtime. "I'm sure your Silly Santa pal is fine. He's probably gone home to see his family. After all, that's what everybody does on Christmas Eve. Now go to sleep so that the real Santa can come and deliver your presents."

Sally and Jayne tried to fall asleep so that Santa could come, but they were just too worried about their missing friend. They were still awake long after Mum and Dad had gone to bed. They were just whispering about how to discover what had happened to Silly Santa, when they heard a magical tinkling sound coming from outside their bedroom window, followed by a familiar sound.

"Yo-ho-ho."

"That sounded just like…" began Jayne.

"…Silly Santa!" finished Sally. Both girls leaped out of bed and rushed over to the window. They looked out, and you can imagine their surprise when they saw Silly Santa flying across the night sky on a sleigh pulled by six reindeer.

Sally and Jayne gasped as the sleigh did a loop-the-loop before pulling up beside their window.

"Yo-ho-ho!" cried Silly Santa. "Didn't I always tell you I was the real thing?" For you see, Silly Santa wasn't silly at all. He was the lovely, kind, funny, real Santa! Sally and Jayne just couldn't believe it.

"Why were you working in the shopping mall?" asked Jayne.

"Ah," smiled Santa. "I like to go out and about to see what kind of presents children want, and which girls and boys are good and which ones aren't. Then I know who really deserves the presents they ask for in the Christmas letters they send to me at the North Pole."

"Oh, dear," wailed Jayne, thinking about the chaos they had caused in the shopping mall that afternoon. "I think we've been bad today."

Santa's eyes began to twinkle.

"Don't worry, little detectives. I know

all about your shopping mall adventures. You didn't mean to be bad."

Then Santa threw back his head and let out a loud rumbling chuckle. His tummy wobbled more than ever, and his bushy white beard shook, too. He laughed so much that soon Sally, Jayne and all the reindeer joined in, too … And that's the last thing Sally and Jayne remembered before they awoke the following morning.

Outside, the sun was shining on the crisp white snow and at the bottom of their beds lay exactly what they had both asked for – two Secret Detective kits! It was Christmas morning at last. Silly Santa was safe and all was well with the world. What a wonderful start to Christmas Day!

Reindeer Elves to the Rescue

by Sue Nicholson

"No, no, no," muttered Toby, the chief toy-making elf in Santa's workshop. He was examining a toy train sitting on his workbench.

"This won't do. This won't do at all!"

He looked down the rows of elves, all hard at work in the workshop making Santa's Christmas toys.

"Dinky! Fingle! Jinx! Come here at once!" he ordered.

Three young elves got up slowly and went to stand in front of Toby.

"Do you recognize this?" asked Toby, holding up the toy train. The three elves nodded glumly.

"The red paint has dripped. That's your fault, Dinky," said Toby sternly. "The wheels aren't straight. That's down to you, Fingle. And just look at the name on the side!" This time he glared at Jinx. "It's spelt wrongly!"

Toby sighed. "What am I going to do with you three?" he asked, shaking his head. "Last week we had a problem with dolls' hair covered in glue. Then you managed to lose the keys for a batch of clockwork mice..."

Sniggering came from an elf sitting at a workbench behind poor Dinky, Fingle and Jinx.

"That will be enough from you, Digget!" called Toby.

Toby looked at the elves standing in front of him.

"Look," he continued kindly. "We have just three weeks until Christmas Eve.

We cannot afford any more mistakes, or the toys won't be finished on time." Dinky began to sniff, trying to hold back her tears.

"We do try," said Jinx.

"And we'll try even harder, we promise!" cried Fingle.

"I know you will," said Toby, "but enough is enough," he continued. "No more toy-making for you three, at least this year. I want you to go down to the stables and see Annie. She's the elf in charge of Santa's reindeer team this year, and she might need some help."

The three elves trooped out. "Ha!" jeered Digget as they filed past. "Toy-making elves who can't make toys! You're better off with the nasty, smelly old reindeer!"

"That Digget is so mean!" sobbed Dinky, as they pushed open the door of the toy-making workshop and went outside.

"What are we going to do?"

"I suppose we had better do what we've been told," sighed Fingle, "...find Annie and help with the reindeer."

"I don't know anything about reindeer," moaned Dinky, as they trudged through the snow, "but they're so beautiful. I don't think they're nasty and smelly like Digget said. Do you, Fingle?"

"No, I like them," replied Fingle.

"Me too," said Jinx. "Maybe it will be fun to look after them – better than toy-making anyway!"

The three elves walked towards the stables where the reindeer lived.

"Ah, just in time to help with the feeding," said a cheerful voice.

"Santa!" cried Dinky. "What are you doing here?"

Santa laughed. "Oh, I'm often down here for a chat with Annie," he replied.

"And I like seeing my beauties," he continued, stroking a reindeer's soft furry neck. "This is Dancer," he said. "Come on, Dancer, say 'hello' to your new friends – Dinky, Fingle and Jinx."

"He's lovely," breathed Fingle. The other reindeer trotted closer. One pushed its soft muzzle into Dinky's hand.

"Oh, that tickles," she laughed.

"That's Donner," chuckled Santa. "And here's Blitzen and Dasher. You'll soon learn their names."

"I know that one," cried Jinx in excitement, pointing to a reindeer with a bright-red nose. "Hello, Rudolph!"

"That's right," smiled Santa. "You've made a good start already. What do you think, Annie?" he said, turning to a kindly-looking elf who had entered the stables.

"Yes," Annie agreed, smiling. "I think

you three will do very well here."

For the next two weeks, the elves worked hard, helping Annie look after the reindeer. They hauled bundles of hay into the feeding troughs, brushed the reindeer's coats until they gleamed, and helped to muck out the stalls. Santa dropped by at

least once a day for a chat and to give tasty treats to the reindeer.

Digget also came by, but only to tease Dinky, Fingle and Jinx.

"What's that nasty pong?" he liked to

shout. "Oh, it's those smelly elves. They're as stinky as the reindeer now!"

"Just ignore him," whispered Fingle to Jinx and Dinky, as they poured water into the reindeer's trough.

"Hmm," said Annie, coming up behind them. "Don't take any notice. His grandfather was just the same. He used to tease me, too, when I first became a reindeer elf."

"Were you a toy-making elf once, too?" asked Dinky.

"That's right," replied Annie. "But I wasn't very good at it," she smiled. "I was much better at taking care of the reindeer. Come on. We'd best fill up the rest of those water troughs; then you can get the reindeer their feed. I'm going to pop over to the toy-making workshop for a word with Toby."

The elves followed Annie into the food

store, chatting happily. None of them saw Digget sneak back into the stable yard and open the stable doors.

When the three elves came back half an hour later, Santa's reindeer had gone!

"We definitely shut the doors," wailed Jinx unhappily.

"I know, but how did they get out?" cried Fingle.

"Come on!" yelled Dinky. "We've got to find them before Annie gets back!"

The three elves ran out of the yard, following the reindeer's hoof prints through the snow. The prints led over a hill, through a small wood, and down to a stream. And there, on the banks of the stream, were hundreds and hundreds of reindeer.

"Oh no! Santa's reindeer must have got mixed up in that big herd!" cried Dinky. "How can we tell which ones are which?"

"Let's try calling them," suggested Jinx.

"That might work."

Together the three elves shouted the reindeer's names.

"Dancer! Prancer! Dasher! Vixen! Comet!"

But it was no use. The elves' tiny voices could not be heard over the noise of the reindeer's hooves.

"We could look for Rudolph's red nose," said Fingle.

"We'll never spot him," sighed Dinky. "There are too many of them!"

"What about getting some of their favourite food?" suggested Jinx.

"Good idea," said Fingle. "Let's try it!" The elves ran back for a bag of Annie's special feed mix and spread it on the ground by the herd. The problem was that ALL the reindeer came over to try some, and the elves had to climb a tree to get out of their way.

"It's no use," cried Jinx.

"I know," said Dinky suddenly. "We'll use Santa's sleigh bells!" The other two elves looked at her, puzzled.

"The reindeer always fly when they hear Santa's magic sleigh bells," she explained. "If we get the bells and jingle them, Santa's reindeer should fly towards the tinkling noise of the bells.

"Brillliant idea!" declared Jinx admiringly. The elves ran back to the stable, grabbed Santa's sleigh bells, and dashed back to the herd. Together they jingled the bells as hard as they could.

Like magic, Santa's reindeer rose up out of the herd and started to fly towards them. The elves ran as fast as they could back to the stable, jingling the bells all the way, with the reindeer following happily behind them.

Santa, Annie, Toby and Digget were

waiting in the stable yard. They watched as the reindeer floated down into their stables, and Annie shut the doors behind them.

"Nice work!" said Santa, approvingly.

"Yes, well done!" smiled Annie.

"And I've got someone here who has an apology to make," said Toby, pushing Digget forwards. "I spotted him opening the gate from my workshop window, but I thought he was helping you and I didn't realise what he was really up to," he explained.

"I'm very sorry," said Digget in a small voice. "I was just having a joke. I didn't think the reindeer would go far."

"That's not really the point, Digget," said Santa sternly. "I can't have elves being mean to each other."

"I promise I won't be mean any more," replied a very sorry-looking Digget.

"That's alright, Digget," said Dinky.

"But you should really get to know the reindeer. They're wonderful, and not smelly at all!"

Santa grinned. "You know, not many elves are good at looking after reindeer. It's a special gift, and I believe you three have it. How would you like to help Annie look after the reindeer all the time? She's told me you make a great team and she'll

be very glad to have you. The reindeer certainly like you, too."

"Yes, please," chorused Dinky, Fingle and Jinx. "We love being reindeer elves! Let's get to work. Christmas is coming!"

Minty's First Snow

by Claire Noonan

It was the night before Christmas and in a little cottage in a small country village, a puppy called Minty was finding out all about the Christmas season from his human, Thomas.

"You see, Minty, on Christmas Eve, Father Christmas visits all the children and gives them each a sack full of presents," Thomas explained. "Father Christmas is a very happy and kind man with a big white beard and he always wears a red suit. He flies through the skies on a sleigh pulled by reindeer and climbs down children's chimneys to deliver presents during the night. On Christmas Day I open all my presents from Father Christmas, then I have a big meal with my whole family, open even more presents, play games and sing carols, and have lots and lots of fun!"

Minty liked the sound of the big meal.

"That means lots of tasty titbits for me," he thought, licking his lips.

"And tomorrow, on Christmas Day, the weatherman on TV says it might snow," Thomas continued as he jumped into bed. "You haven't seen snow before, Minty, but I know you'll love it. Snow is little flakes of white stuff that float down from the sky and it's brilliant because you can build snowmen with it and play snowballs."

Thomas pulled the covers up around him. Minty curled up in his usual place on the foot of Thomas's bed and soon they were both fast asleep.

During the night, Minty woke up. He'd been dreaming about food as usual and he was hoping it was breakfast time.

He nuzzled back the curtain with his nose and looked out of the bedroom window. He could hardly believe his eyes. It was still dark but he could see that something rather strange had happened to the world. Everything had turned white! Big white flakes were falling out of the sky and covering everything in sight.

Minty padded out of the bedroom and crept downstairs to investigate. Because he was still a little puppy he could just about squeeze outside through the catflap. He knew he really shouldn't, but he badly wanted to see what was going on in the garden. Outside, the moonlight danced on the white stuff and made it sparkle like tiny crystals. The crystals hung to roofs and trees and had turned the garden into a big white carpet.

"This must be the snow that Thomas was telling me about," he thought.

"I wonder what it feels like." Minty carefully put one paw in the white stuff and yelped with surprise.

"Brrr! It's freezing!" he gasped. He took a few more steps into the garden and looked up into the sky with his tongue hanging out. A big, wet flake of snow landed on his tongue. Plop! It tasted like cold water.

"This snow stuff is nothing to be afraid of!" he barked excitedly. He rolled around in the snow and shook himself so all the flakes flew off in different directions. Thomas was right. Snow really was great fun, just as he had said.

It was far too early to wake Thomas up, so Minty decided to go and see his friends at Crippen's Farm. They were bound to want to play in the snow with him. He trotted to the bottom of the garden, pushed open the garden gate with his paw and raced over the field towards the farm.

"Wake up, cows!" he cried, as he raced into the cowshed. He was running so fast that he knocked over a milk churn. CRASH! The cows all woke up with grumpy 'moo' noises.

"Whatever is going on? What's that noise?" they grumbled.

"It's snowing!" panted Minty. "Do you want to come outside and play?"

"No!" they snapped. "We most certainly do NOT want to play in that horrible, cold stuff. Go away and let us sleep, please!"

So, with his tail between his legs, Minty slunk out of the cowshed. He decided to go and see the horses, Trigger and Flash, to find out if they wanted to play with him instead. The snow had stopped falling now, but there was still a thick covering on the ground.

"Hello, Trigger! Hello, Flash!" barked Minty as he padded into the stables. "Do you want to come outside and play in the snow?"

"Neigh! Maybe later, Minty," yawned a sleepy Trigger.

"It's far too early to play," mumbled Flash, sleepily.

Poor Minty. No one wanted to play with him.

"I'll go home and wait for Thomas to wake up then," he barked sulkily. "He will definitely want to play in the snow with me!"

Minty walked out of the stables and looked around. Just behind the farm there was a big wood and Minty suddenly had an idea. Maybe he wouldn't go home just yet. There were bound to be lots of woodland animals that would like to play in the snow with him.

Minty searched everywhere in the wood but he couldn't find any animals to play with. They were all enjoying their winter sleep, curled up in their cosy homes.

"I may as well go home then," sighed Minty sadly. He looked around, trying to remember which way he had come from. He raced this way and that but, with the snow covering the branches of the trees and bushes, everything looked the same. Minty suddenly realized that he didn't know his way out of the wood. He was lost!

Just then, Minty heard a jingling sound in the distance. 'Jingle, jangle, jingle jangle,' it went. It sounded just like bells.

Minty pricked up his ears and listened hard. The sound seemed to be coming from behind him. He turned around and ran towards it.

Soon, he saw where it was coming from. Down by a lake in the middle of the wood, stood a man dressed in a red suit. He was surrounded by strange-looking animals, each with a smart red collar and a bell around their neck. The animals were drinking from the lake and as they lowered their long, graceful necks, their bells rang.

One of the animals was standing near a sleigh piled high with sacks. Minty knew it was a sleigh because Thomas kept one in the shed at home. But this one was much, much bigger. It was nearly as big as Thomas's parents' car!

Minty crept forwards.

"Can you help me?" he asked one of the funny-looking animals. "I'm lost. I live at Thomas's house, over the field from Crippen's Farm. Do you know which way I should go?"

The animal shook its head.

"Er, I hope you don't mind me asking," continued Minty, "but what sort of animal are you? By the way, I like your collar with the bell. It's very smart."

"Why, I'm a reindeer, of course!" the reindeer declared. "I'm afraid I don't really know all the names of the houses around here so I can't help you. I'm sorry."

Minty slumped into the snow and began to howl. He'd been so looking forward to spending his first Christmas with Thomas. Now he'd never get to play in the snow with his friend or eat all the tasty titbits from the Christmas feast.

The reindeer felt very sorry for the poor little dog, and tried to think of a way to make him smile again. Then he had a brainwave.

"I know what to do, little dog," he cried. "Look at the snow!"

Minty lifted his head and looked around. He couldn't see anything very exciting, just snow, snow and more snow.

"Your paws have made pawprints in the snow," said the reindeer. "All you need to do is follow the trail right back to the beginning and you'll find yourself back at home. I promise!"

Just then, the man in the red suit gave a shout and jumped back into the sledge. The reindeer all trotted towards him, and with a 'jingle, jangle, jingle, jangle', the sleigh soared into the air and flew out of sight.

Minty could hardly believe his eyes. Had he just imagined all that? He looked at the snow and there, sure enough, lay a trail of little doggie pawprints. He barked excitedly and began to follow them. He ran round and round the wood, following the trail past bushes, trees and hedgerows until finally he popped out of the wood and saw Crippen's Farm in front of him.

He followed the trail back through the stables, through the cowsheds, across the field, through the garden gate and right to Thomas's back door.

Minty quietly crept into Thomas's house and padded back up the stairs and into Thomas's bedroom, where he curled up in his usual position at the foot of Thomas's bed.

He yawned and closed his eyes. He had been on an exciting adventure and now he felt very tired indeed.

When Minty woke up next morning, Thomas was already up and very excited. He was opening a pile of presents that somebody had left in the night.

"Minty, Father Christmas has left one for you!" he cried, and he handed Minty a little parcel. Inside there was a smart red collar with a tiny bell on it, just like the ones he'd seen the funny animals wearing,

down by the lake.

"Well I never," thought Minty. "I wonder how Father Christmas knew what I wanted."

He never worked it out. Can you?

Catch That Letter

by Gaby Goldsack

One Christmas Eve, the icy North Wind blew briskly against the walls of Santa's workshop. But the little elves inside took no notice. They were far too busy to worry about the weather. There were many things still to be done before Santa could leave to deliver presents around the world.

The busiest elf of all was Felix, the letter-sorting elf. His job was to sort out all the letters boys and girls sent to Santa telling him what they wanted for Christmas. It wasn't an easy task. This year there had been so many letters that Felix had taken on an assistant called Zack, but they were still hard at work on

Christmas Eve. Finally, it looked like their job was almost finished when something quite unexpected happened. Felix had just pulled out the last letter from the last mailbag, when the window burst open and the North Wind blew in and snatched the letter from his grasp.

"I'll bet you can't catch it again!" whistled the North Wind. He blew the letter high into the air and swept it straight out of the window.

"I must get that letter back," cried Felix.

"Does it really matter?" called Zack. "It's just one letter in a million."

"It might be one in a million, but each and every one of those letters is important," cried Felix, as he rushed out of the door. "They contain the hopes and dreams of children. See you later!"

Felix raced across the snow after the

wind-blown letter. He followed it round and round the giant fir trees and into the reindeer's stables. Still the North Wind blew the letter on and on.

"Oh, no," groaned Felix, as he watched the letter fly between Dancer the reindeer's legs and disappear out of the window. "It looks like it's gone for good now."

"What's gone for good?" asked the startled reindeer.

As quickly as he could, Felix explained about the letter stolen by the North Wind. As Dancer listened, his ears pricked up and he began to kick up his hooves excitedly.

"Don't worry," he cried. "Jump on my back and we'll catch the letter before you can say 'jingle bells'."

Felix jumped on the kind reindeer's back and together they raced across the windswept snow. They saw the North Wind sweep the letter upwards, until it disappeared above the fluffy clouds.

"Hold on tight," cried Dancer, as suddenly, and most unexpectedly, they began to rise up into the sky. Felix closed his eyes tightly as they rose higher and higher until, when he opened them once more, they were soaring way above the clouds. Just ahead of them, Felix could see the letter twirling and whirling around.

They flew over mountains and oceans but still the letter blew on and on. Then, just as Felix was about to give up hope, the wind dropped and the letter plummeted towards the ground. Dancer put his head down and zoomed after it, with Felix clinging on as tightly as he could. They burst through the clouds just in time to see the letter flutter onto the balcony of a little flat. Dancer, who was going too fast to stop prettily, crash-landed beside it.

Without stopping to worry about

bumps or bruises, Felix picked himself up and snatched up the letter. He clutched it to his chest and looked around wildly. At any moment, he expected the North Wind to snatch it from his grasp. Then he looked into the sky and saw the smiling wind waving goodbye. It seemed that the North Wind had blown the letter where he wanted it to go, and now it was time for him to leave.

"Bye Felix! That chase was fun!" he whistled, as he disappeared from sight.

As soon as Felix was sure that the North Wind had gone, he held out the letter and read it very carefully.

Dear Santa,

I don't really need anything for Christmas but it would be great if you could bring my little sister, Emily, the doll she wants. It has golden hair and looks like a princess.

Many thanks,

Tom

PS. Emily has been very good all year, and I have tried my best.

Felix had just finished reading the letter when he heard voices coming from inside the flat. It sounded like children. Felix and Dancer crept over and pressed their noses up against the window. Inside, they could see a little girl and a boy decorating a tiny Christmas tree with homemade decorations. It was obvious that they were very poor. The children were dressed in patched and threadbare clothes and the tree they stood around barely reached their knees. But they both looked excited and happy.

"Oh, Tom, it's a perfect tree," cried the little girl, clapping her hands with glee. "Do you think Santa will leave a doll beneath it tonight?"

"Of course, he will," replied the little boy.

"And do you think he'll leave you a bicycle, as well? I know you'd really like one," added Tom's sister.

"Oh, never mind about that," smiled Tom.

Outside the window, Dancer and Felix

looked at each other and gasped.

"It's the boy who wrote the letter," whispered Dancer. "I think the North Wind brought us here on purpose. He wanted us to see this."

"Yes," agreed Felix. "And it sounds like Tom does want something for Christmas, after all, but he was too unselfish to ask for it. Come on, let's get back to the North Pole straight away. There's not a moment to lose."

Dancer soared into the sky and raced towards home as swiftly as he could. Soon he was making a perfect landing beside Santa's parcel-packed sleigh. Dusk was falling and it was nearly time for the sleigh to leave. While Dancer quickly took his place at the head of the sleigh, Felix went to find Santa.

When Santa had read the letter and heard what Dancer and Felix had seen at the flat, he tugged at his beard thoughtfully.

"I know that little boy," he said slowly. "He has been very good all year long. He looks after his little sister, always does as he's told, and helps his mum whenever he can. I think we should certainly make sure that he has something nice to unwrap on Christmas morning. Quickly, see if you can find a princess doll, while I go and see if we've got any bicycles left."

With the help of his trusty assistant, Zack, Felix soon had a pretty doll and a smart red bicycle beautifully wrapped and carefully stowed aboard Santa's sleigh. Then, in a flurry of magical snowflakes, Santa and his reindeer raced away across the night sky to deliver everybody's Christmas presents

Felix was so tired after his letter-chasing adventure that he headed straight to bed and fell into a deep, deep sleep.

He dreamed of flying letters and

reindeer. The next thing he knew, somebody was shaking him awake.

"Go away, Zack," Felix muttered, thinking it was his assistant waking him up to go to work.

"Ho, ho, ho!" laughed a voice in reply.

"Wakey, wakey! It's Christmas Day."

The voice came from a beaming Santa, standing beside Felix's bed. Felix shot out of bed and stood to attention.

"I'm so sorry, Santa! Have I overslept? Have I forgotten to do something?"

"Relax," laughed Santa. "I've brought you a present. I thought you deserved it after all your hard work." He handed Felix a parcel that looked a bit like a giant tube of sweets. Felix ripped off the wrapping paper and found a shiny golden telescope inside, for looking at the night stars.

"Wow! Thank you," cried Felix. "I've always wanted one of these."

"It's not just any old telescope," said Santa, with a twinkle in his eye. "Go on, look through it and see for yourself."

Felix squinted through the eyeglass and gasped. This was indeed a magical telescope. Through it Felix could see all the way to Tom's flat. He could see Tom proudly polishing the bell of his new bicycle. Tom's sister Emily was playing with her new doll. Behind them he could see their parents unwrapping an enormous hamper full of biscuits, cakes, fruit, and the biggest turkey you could possibly imagine. It was a special extra gift from Santa to the whole family.

Felix threw his arms around Santa's tummy and laughed.

"Come on, then, little Felix. You'd better get up, or you'll miss all the Christmas fun."

Felix couldn't wait to tell Dancer all about what had happened. Just as soon as he was able to, he went outside to the stables. Dancer knew that the children had got their presents, because he had shown Santa exactly where to deliver them the night before. He was delighted that

everything had turned out well. Then, just as Felix was about to leave, the stable door blew open and they both heard the whistling voice of the clever North Wind.

"Woooooooo! Wooooooo! Happy Christmas everyone!"

The Christmas Fairy

by Claire Noonan

Down in a sunlit clearing in Bluebell Wood, the fairies of Fairy Glen were gathering for their annual meeting. Every year, the Queen of the Fairies set a challenge and the winner was awarded the top honour… to be crowned the Christmas Fairy and sit on top of the biggest, prettiest Christmas tree in the human kingdom.

"I wonder who will win this year," said Buttercup excitedly.

"Oh, it'll be Rose, I should imagine," replied Daisy. "She's the prettiest fairy in Fairy Glen so she's sure to win!"

"It takes more than a pretty face to win the honour of being the Christmas

Fairy!" exclaimed Marigold. "You have to be incredibly smart to pass the Queen's special challenge."

"Imagine how proud the winner would feel, sitting on top of that beautiful human Christmas tree!" sighed Daisy. The other fairies all nodded wistfully.

Little Daisy thought of herself as a boring ordinary fairy, though she tried very hard at everything she did. She always helped the other fairies with their chores and she was especially good at rocking the baby fairies to sleep in their rose-petal cots. But she didn't feel she had any chance of winning the challenge. It didn't stop her daydreaming, though, and she was just imagining what it would be like on top of the tree, when she heard the Queen of the Fairies clapping her hands loudly.

"Silence please!" she cried. All the fairies stopped chattering and a hush descended on the wood. "Thank you all for coming. As you know, every year I set a challenge and the winner is awarded the top fairy honour – to be crowned the Christmas Fairy. This year's challenge is especially hard. I want you to find the Christmas Spirit by midnight."

With that, the Queen stepped inside her horse-chestnut shell coach and six shiny black beetles pulled her coach away into the night.

The fairies all looked at one another in dismay.

"Whatever is the Christmas Spirit?" gasped Buttercup.

"Well, we'd better stop nattering and start looking right now! Good luck everybody!" cried Marigold, and she flew off busily, along with all the other fairies except Daisy. She hadn't begun her search yet because she was thinking hard. She remembered her great-grandmother telling her about a wise old fairy, called Ragwort, who lived in the Dark Forest and who knew the answers to all kinds of strange questions. Ragwort would be sure to know how to find the Christmas Spirit. But the Dark Forest was a scary place that lay in the middle of two hills right on the other side of the fairy kingdom.

Daisy quickly packed an acorn rucksack with some nectar juice and three slices of blackberry cake and she set off for the Dark Forest. She flew for miles and miles, over rivers and lakes, woods and forests, until finally her wings ran out of flutter and she had to stop for a rest. She swooped down into a grassy clearing and lay her head on what she thought was a smooth rock.

"Oi!" said the rock. "Watch where you're sticking those wings, fairy girl!"

Daisy jumped up in surprise. The rock turned out to be a rather bad-tempered crow with a damaged wing.

"Oh, I'm terribly sorry, Mr Crow, Sir!" stammered Daisy. "I thought you were a rock!"

"By my feathers! A rock indeed, caw haw haw!" the crow giggled. "You are a funny fairy!"

Just then, Daisy noticed the crow's damaged wing. She didn't really have time to stop and help the poor crow, but she didn't think twice. "Let me sew up your wound and then you'll be able to fly again," she exclaimed.

The crow looked at Daisy in surprise.

"Thank you!" he gasped.

So Daisy set to work. With a pine needle and a strand of her own hair, she slowly and carefully stitched up the bird's wing. As she sewed, she told the crow about the challenge that the Queen of Fairies had set and how she needed to find the wise old fairy, Ragwort, so that she could ask for her help.

"Christmas Spirit, eh?" pondered the crow. "I'm afraid I've never heard of that. But I have heard some of the woodland creatures talk of Ragwort. She lives in the Dark Forest."

"Do you know how I can find her house?" asked Daisy hopefully.

"No, but the mermaids of the Blue Lagoon know where she lives," said the crow, "and now you have mended my wing, I can fly you there!" So the little fairy climbed onto the crow's back and off they flew. The crow had huge wings that could fly a lot faster than Daisy's little ones, and they were soon soaring over the beautiful Blue Lagoon. Daisy could see lots of mermaids sitting on rocks, splashing their tails in the water and singing as they combed their long, golden hair.

The crow landed on a rock by the side of the lagoon and Daisy raced over to ask the mermaids if they could help her.

"Of course we'll help you!" said one of the mermaids. "Ragwort lives in a beautiful red toadstool next to the third oak on the left, by the lake in the Dark Forest."

Daisy hugged the mermaid tightly.

"Thank you so much!" she cried as she raced back to the crow and jumped onto his back. They headed off for the Dark Forest, over the Blue Lagoon and past a big waterfall. Daisy looked down and suddenly noticed a mermaid whose tail was stuck between two rocks high

above the waterfall.

"Please stop for a moment, crow," Daisy shouted. "We must help that poor mermaid. If she doesn't get out soon she will become very weak and ill!"

"But if we stop to help her, you may

not find the Christmas Spirit in time. Look, the sky is getting dark now. It's nearly night-time," the crow pointed out.

"Never mind about that," Daisy declared. So they swooped down and Daisy gently pulled the mermaid's tail out from between the rocks.

"Thank you so much!" smiled the mermaid as she splashed her tail happily. Moments later, Daisy and the crow were back in the air.

"I'm afraid I will have to leave you at the edge of the Dark Forest, as crows are not allowed inside," said the crow as they neared the forest's edge.

"That's alright. I'll be fine by myself," whispered Daisy, trying hard to feel brave. She said goodbye to the crow and flew on alone.

The Dark Forest certainly was dark. It looked very frightening and the little fairy felt quite scared. She flew around and around, looking for an oak tree near a lake. The forest was getting more and more gloomy, and Daisy knew that midnight must soon be approaching. There was no way she was going to find the Christmas Spirit in time.

Poor Daisy felt sad and exhausted. She realised that she was also very hungry and thirsty and she remembered the nectar juice and cake that she'd packed in her acorn bag. She fluttered down to the ground.

Just at that moment, a wizened old woman appeared as if from nowhere.

"Hello pretty fairy," she cackled. "Could you spare some food for an old beggar woman?" Even though she was incredibly hungry, Daisy felt sorry for the old lady, who looked as though she hadn't had a decent meal for months. She gave her all her cake and juice and, as the woman ate, Daisy told her about the Queen's challenge.

"I don't think I'm ever going to find Ragwort's house," said Daisy at the end of her tale, "and I think it's too late. I knew a boring ordinary fairy like me wouldn't be able to find the Christmas Spirit." The old lady looked at the fairy and laughed. Just a little giggle at first, then a chuckle, then a huge guffaw. She laughed and laughed as though her sides would burst!

"I AM Ragwort!" she laughed. "And you HAVE found the Christmas Spirit! It is something that lives inside you. It's not an object but a feeling of kindness that you have for all those around you. You see, even though you were in a hurry to complete your challenge, you still found the time to repair the crow's wing and rescue the mermaid. Then you gave me your food and drink, even though you were thirsty and hungry yourself. The Queen of the Fairies told me about her challenge and she knew that it would take a very special fairy to come looking for me and pass the test!" With that, Ragwort turned into a beautiful forest fairy.

Daisy rubbed her eyes in amazement.

"D-do you mean I've passed the challenge?" she stammered.

"You certainly have!" said another voice. Out of the bushes appeared the Queen of Fairies. She was carrying the most beautiful golden crown, studded with sparkling emeralds, rubies and diamonds that glimmered in the light of the moon.

"This year, you will be the Christmas Fairy," she declared as she put the crown on Daisy's head.

So, on Christmas Eve, a very kind and very brave Christmas Fairy sat

proudly on top of the biggest and sparkliest Christmas tree in the human kingdom. It was Daisy, who really wasn't boring or ordinary after all!

You're in the Team!

by Kath Jewitt

Vincent the reindeer was the busiest reindeer in his herd. Or so it seemed. For every time one of the other reindeer asked him for help, Vincent was always too busy to lend a hand.

"I'm sorry!" he would say. "I'd love to help, but I'm just too busy. I don't have a moment to spare."

In fact, Vincent wasn't really busy at all. He was just too lazy to be bothered. But he wasn't going to tell the rest of the herd that. It was much easier to pretend he had other things to do.

One day, Vincent was extremely busy doing nothing at all, when Silver, the oldest reindeer in his herd, came to find him.

"Hurry up!" he called. "You'll miss all the excitement. Santa Claus will be here any minute."

"Santa!" exclaimed Vincent. "Why is he coming to visit?"

"He wants to choose a new reindeer to join his special team," replied Silver. "The winner will help deliver all the presents on Christmas Eve. It's a great honour!"

Vincent knew all about Santa Claus, but he had never met him before.

"I wonder what he's really like," he exclaimed. "I can't wait to meet him."

Then Vincent had a worrying thought. "If I go to meet Santa, he might choose me for his team, and I don't want that. It sounds like hard work!"

So Vincent came up with a clever plan.

"I'll hide behind a tree," he decided. "That way, I'll see Santa, but he won't see me." So off he went to find a good hiding place.

When Santa Claus arrived, there was great excitement.

Everyone (apart from Vincent) was determined to make a good impression. And everyone (apart from Vincent) was desperate to be chosen.

"Pick me, Santa!" they all begged, doing their best to look big and strong. "Please!"

Santa held up his hand for silence. "What a fine herd of reindeer!" he cried. "I would be delighted to have any of you on my team. But I'm looking for a special reindeer this year. Someone a little different …"

As Santa spoke, he saw something moving in the trees. He looked more closely, and then beamed.

"In fact," he twinkled, "I'm looking for

someone exactly like … YOU!" He pointed at Vincent.

"Me?" gasped Vincent, peeping out. "You don't want me, do you?"

"I do!" replied Santa. "You're exactly who I'm looking for."

"But I'm very busy on Christmas Eve," mumbled Vincent. Santa didn't seem to hear him. "Come on, now," he boomed. "There's no need to be shy. You're perfect for the job."

Of course, Vincent didn't agree at all, but he didn't dare say a word.

The other reindeer watched enviously, as Santa harnessed Vincent to his sleigh and climbed aboard.

"Giddy up, Vincent!" he cried, flicking the reins. "The North Pole, please!"

Vincent frowned sulkily.

"It's not fair!" he grumbled under his breath. But he didn't want to look silly in front of the others, so he put his head down and pulled with all his might. HEAVE!

It was hard work. Very hard work. But just as Vincent was about to give up, the sleigh gave a jerk. Then it began to glide forward.

"Good work," cheered Santa, as they pulled away. "I knew you could do it."

"Harrumph," snorted Vincent rudely, though he secretly felt rather pleased. "It's not that hard," he thought, as they raced along. "I don't know why I was worried."

Vincent's good mood didn't last. It was a long way to Santa's Grotto, and it was exhausting pulling the sleigh by himself. By the time they arrived home, Vincent was out of breath, tired and very grumpy. Strangely, Santa didn't seem to notice. He just patted Vincent on the back and gave him a juicy carrot.

"Well done," he said, and led him to

the stable.

Vincent settled down in the straw to munch his carrot.

"That was hard work," he yawned, as he closed his eyes. "But I did it!" Then he fell fast asleep.

Vincent hadn't been asleep for long

when he was woken by loud noises. The rest of Santa's reindeer had returned.

"Hello," called one, poking his head into Vincent's stall. "Welcome to the team!"

"Go away," snapped Vincent, crossly. "I'm sleeping." Then he turned his back, and closed his eyes again.

"How rude!" snorted the other reindeer. "I wonder why Santa chose him?"

"Maybe Santa felt sorry for him," said another. And they all laughed.

"Santa has a good reason for everything he does," interrupted a voice. It was Rudolph, Santa's kindest reindeer. "Now hush, or you'll wake him up again," he whispered. But Vincent wasn't asleep. He was listening to every word.

"Why did Santa choose me?" he wondered. "I'm not big and strong, and I'm certainly not helpful."

The more Vincent thought about

it, the more ashamed he felt. Until he remembered what Rudolph had said.

"Santa must have chosen me for a reason," he decided. "If Santa thinks I'm good enough, I must be."

From that moment on, Vincent couldn't wait for Christmas Eve to come. "I'll prove that Santa was right about me," he cried. "I'll work harder than anyone!"

And that's exactly what he did. When Christmas Eve finally arrived, Vincent was the star of the team. He was more enthusiastic than Dancer, faster than Dasher and Comet, and stronger than Donner or Blitzen, Vixen or Cupid. He was even as helpful as Rudolph!

The other reindeer were delighted, but no one was more pleased than Santa himself.

"We couldn't have managed without your help," he told an exhausted, but

happy Vincent. "I knew I'd made the right choice."

Vincent felt so proud, he thought he would burst.

"Thank you, Santa," he beamed. "But why did you choose me?"

Santa smiled. "Because I knew just how helpful you could be," he replied, "if only you had the chance to find out for yourself!"

The Snowstorm Surprise

by Kath Jewitt

Ella and Luke MacDonald lived on a farm with their mum and dad. The farm was so high up in the hills, it sometimes felt like they lived at the top of the world. It was miles from anywhere, but Ella and Luke didn't mind. They thought it was a wonderful place to live. For most of the year they played outside, exploring the hills and spotting the wildlife that lived around them.

In winter, though, when icy winds whistled and the ground was frozen hard, it wasn't quite so much fun. Sometimes, when the weather was really bad, the family was snowed in for days on end. Even the TV wouldn't work sometimes! Then there was nothing to do but argue and wait for the snow to melt.

Of course, winter wasn't all bad. There was always Christmas! Ella and Luke loved everything to do with it. The loved writing Christmas lists, making decorations, going on shopping trips to the big city, and the smell of spicy biscuits drifting through the house …

Best of all was Christmas Eve, when Ella, Luke and Dad went to choose the Christmas tree. Then Mum got down the decorations from the attic, and all the neighbours came round for a tree-decorating party. Everyone looked forward to it, so imagine Ella and Luke's disappointment when the tree party was cancelled one Christmas Eve.

Mum was waiting for them at the gate, when they arrived home with the Christmas tree.

"A big snowstorm is coming," she told Dad. "I just heard on the radio. I'm sorry kids, but there's no time for the party. We have to bring the animals into the barn right away."

Ella and Luke's hearts sank, but they didn't complain. They knew the animals could freeze in the snow if they stayed outside.

"Don't worry, Mum," said Ella, as they left the tree by the barn. "The party can wait." Mum gave them both a hug.

"Maybe we can decorate the tree later," she smiled. "Now go and wrap up warmly. We all need to help!"

Dad hooked up the trailer to the tractor, while Ella and Luke found their snow gear.

"Mum and I will fetch the cows and sheep in the top field," Dad told them. "Can you two get the barn ready? Then you need to bring in your ponies."

Ella and Luke waved their parents goodbye, then went to get the barn ready. Luke spread out fresh hay, while Ella filled the troughs with clean water. When they had finished, they brought in their ponies, Gingernut and Hobnob, from the paddock.

"It's getting windier," shivered Luke. "The snowstorm will be here soon."

The family worked hard, until they all felt frozen to the bone. And all the while, the wind blew stronger and stronger, until tiny flecks of snow began to whirl round the farm. Before they had finished it was night-time.

"I hope Mum and Dad are OK," worried Ella, looking at the time. Just then, they heard the sound of the tractor.

"We've just got the last lot of sheep in," Dad declared. "And just in time! It's really blowing a blizzard up there."

At last they had finished!

"It's not been much of a Christmas Eve!" said Mum later, as they all sat by the fire. "We haven't even decorated the tree."

"It's too late for that now," said Dad, "but at least the animals are safe. Now, let's get to bed, or Santa will be here!"

"I hope he'll be alright in the storm," worried Ella, peering out at the swirling snow. "It must be freezing for him up there in his sleigh!"

"We could leave him a flask of hot chocolate," suggested Luke. "That would warm him up."

Mum smiled. "Good idea," she said. "Then it REALLY is time for bed. We've got to be up early to feed the animals – Christmas or no Christmas!"

It had been an exhausting day, and Ella and Luke fell asleep as soon as their heads hit the pillow. Outside the wind whistled, and the snowstorm raged.

They had been asleep for quite some time, when suddenly both children awoke with a start. A loud racket was coming

from the barn.

'Baa! Moo! Oink! Neigh!' The animals were going crazy!

"Do you think we should go and wake Mum and Dad?" asked Luke, worriedly.

Then, just as suddenly as the noise had started, everything went quiet. Ella tried to peer through the snow-covered window, but she couldn't see a thing.

"Let's not wake them," she decided, climbing back into bed. "They were tired out, and we've all got to be up early to feed the animals."

When Ella and Luke awoke on Christmas morning, bright sunlight was streaming through the curtains. They leapt out of bed, and bounded over to the window. Overnight, the whole world had turned white! They rushed into their parents' room to wake them.

"Merry Christmas, Mum and Dad!" they yelled.

"Merry Christmas," yawned Dad sleepily. He opened his eyes and checked the clock.

"Oh no," he cried, throwing back the

covers. "We've overslept! We need to feed the animals. They must be starving!" The whole family got dressed as quickly as they could, and rushed over to the barn.

"It won't take long if we all help," said Mum, as she opened the barn door. "Then we can have our breakfast."

But the MacDonald family was in for a surprise.

The animals had already been fed! Every animal had fresh food, and that wasn't all. Their Christmas tree was now standing tall and proud in the middle of the barn. Underneath it there were mountains of presents.

"Mum! Dad! Did you do this?" gasped Ella and Luke. But Mr and Mrs MacDonald were just as amazed.

Suddenly, Luke spotted an empty thermos flask, sitting on a hay bale.

"Look!" he cried. "It's the drink we

made for Santa last night. He must have left it behind in the barn!"

"So that's why all the animals made such a noise last night," exclaimed Ella. "Santa did all this for us and our animals were just saying "thank you!"

The Missing Elf

by Hettie Bingham

It was an icy day and the trees were white with frost. Mia and Louis heard it crunching under their feet as they followed their dog Jack through the park. He had rushed off to chase a stick, but now he had forgotten all about that and had started sniffing around in a border of bushes. By the time they caught up with him, the children's ears and noses were glowing with cold.

"I hope it snows this Christmas," said Louis, "and I hope Santa brings me a sledge so I can go whizzing down the hill on it. Wheee!"

"Well I hope Santa brings me a painting set," added Mia, "...and a tea set too, so we can have tea parties whenever we like." As Mia and Louis chattered on about the gifts, Jack began to bark and scratch the frozen ground with his paw.

"Come on, boy! Here's a dog biscuit for you," offered Mia as she tried to calm him down. But Jack kept on sniffing and barking.

"Maybe he has found something in the bushes," said Louis. "Let's have a look." Louis and Mia crouched down to take a closer look. At first they couldn't see a thing.

"There's nothing there," sighed Louis. But then, just as they were about to get up, something made a rustling noise.

"Perhaps it's a little bird who can't fly," suggested Mia. "We could help it!" Louis gently parted the branches of the bush. There, standing under the fronds was, not an injured bird, but an elf. Yes, that's right…an ELF!

At first, the children were so amazed that they couldn't speak. They just stared and stared at the poor little elf. He was shivering and blue with cold. By his side was what looked like a half-eaten acorn. The elf seemed as surprised as they did.

"Er, hi," said Mia. "I think we need to get you out of the cold."

The elf nodded. His teeth were chattering so much he couldn't speak.

So Mia gently scooped him up and put him in her pocket. They rushed back across the park to their home, with Mia being as careful as she could not to jiggle the poor elf around.

"Wipe your feet!" called Louis and Mia's mum as they all spilled through the door. "Did you have a nice walk?" she added, but they didn't reply. They were too busy charging up the stairs to Mia's room.

Once they arrived they shut the door firmly behind them.

Eyes wide with excitement, Mia slowly put her hand inside her pocket and helped out the tiny elf. He was now a lot less blue and was looking healthier by the minute in the warmth of her bedroom.

"Are you real?" whispered Louis.

"Well I'm not a dream, if that's what you mean!" answered the elf rather indignantly.

"He means are you a real elf?" asked Mia kindly. "It's just that we've never seen one before."

"I'm a real elf alright. My name is Finbar," replied the elf proudly, "and I'm not just any old elf either. I'm one of Santa's helpers!"

If Mia and Louis had been excited before, they were now totally thrilled. They began bombarding Finbar with questions.

"Does Santa really know all the children in the world? Does he know our names? Do you know what he's bringing us this year?"

The children were so full of questions they didn't notice that Finbar was looking sadder and sadder.

"I want a painting set and Louis wants a sledge," continued Mia, "a nice big sledge because Jack will want a ride on it and so will...Oh!"

Mia suddenly stopped talking. She had finally noticed how unhappy Finbar seemed. A tear was rolling down his little face.

"Whatever is the matter?" gasped Louis. "Why are you crying?"

"Because I'm lost," blurted out the miserable elf, "and I've got to get back to Santa. It's our busiest time of year!"

"We're so sorry," Mia declared. "We

were so interested in finding out about our presents that we didn't stop to think about how you might be feeling."

"Or what you were doing all alone and shivering in the park," added Louis. "Tell us all about it."

Mia wrapped one of her doll's blankets around Finbar and soon he had stopped

crying. He told his new friends the whole story of how he had ended up in the park. He had been working extra-hard at Santa's Grotto, packing toys. But everyone needs a break sometimes, and Finbar thought he would just pop outside to get some fresh air. He was a little bit sleepy, and thought he'd take a nap on the back of Santa's sleigh, in the soft empty sacks.

What Finbar didn't notice was that Santa's reindeer team were about to set off for a practice run. Santa's reindeer team practise quite a lot in the run up to Christmas, so they won't make any mistakes on the big night. When Finbar woke up, ready to go back to work, he found that he was in the air!

The sleigh ride was terrific: those reindeer really knew how to fly! They looped-the-loop, landed and took off again without a sound. Then they had landed in a park, Mia and Louis's park. It had looked so inviting by the light of a beautiful moon. Finbar had hopped down from the sleigh and scurried into the bushes to look for acorns, a favourite food for elves, and he had found quite a few. As he chomped away happily, he thought his little jaunt was going rather well, and he was imagining what he would tell all his elf friends about it when he returned.

It was then that Finbar had realized his big mistake. The reindeer team had no idea he was on the trip, and he looked up just in time to see the sleigh sailing off into the night, leaving a trail of magic dust behind it. He was stranded and lost.

"And then we came along and found you!" exclaimed Mia.

"Don't worry, Finbar," Louis said. "We'll think of a way to get you back home to Santa."

Mia and Louis started thinking hard. They made lots of suggestions, but none of them sounded as if they would work, until

eventually Mia had a very clever idea.

"Louis, do you remember what Mum always tells us when we go out shopping?" asked Mia.

"Of course I do," Louis replied, sounding slightly puzzled. "She always tells us that, if we get lost we must stay in the place where we last saw her, and she'll come and look for us."

"Well that's what Finbar should do. Someone must have noticed that he's gone missing by now. Maybe they'll figure out what has happened and come looking for him!" Mia declared. Finbar wasn't so sure, but it was the only decent idea they had, so the three of them set to work making their clever plan.

They knew that, every evening, Mia and Louis's Dad took Jack for a walk in the park. That evening, Finbar would hide in Jack's shaggy fur and jump off his back when they arrived at the border of bushes.

It was not long before they heard Dad call upstairs to Jack.

"Walkies!"

Mia made sure that Finbar was wrapped up warm in her doll's coat. Then the little elf sat on Jack's back, holding on tightly. Louis and Mia said their goodbyes to their new friend.

"I hope you get back safely," said Mia as she buttoned up the tiny coat. "And don't worry. We'll be back first thing in the morning to make sure you've gone."

"Yes, and sorry we were so selfish before. Our presents really don't matter as long as you get back safely," added Louis.

"Thank you," said Finbar, though he still looked a little bit worried. He really wasn't sure if this was going to work.

Mia and Louis pressed their faces against the window watching Jack and Dad walking away from the house, until they were out of sight. Once in the park, Jack knew just what to do and raced over to the bushes. Finbar jumped off and hid in the undergrowth, before Dad could notice a thing. Now all he had to do was wait.

Soon it was dark and cold.

"What if Mia was wrong? What if nobody comes to find me?" thought Finbar, and he began to shiver. Large flakes of snow had started to fall and he watched as they began to settle on the grass. Then, when the poor lost elf had almost given up hope, he noticed a star that seemed to be shining extra-brightly. As he watched, the star grew bigger and bigger, and then he realized it was not a star. It was Santa's sleigh! It flew closer and closer until he could hear the reindeer bells jingling, and he could see Santa himself sitting there, large as life. The sleigh glided down and landed gently.

Finbar ran out from the bushes as fast as he could. He was frightened that he would go unnoticed and that the sleigh would take off before his little legs could reach it.

"Santa! Santa! I'm here! It's me, Finbar the present-packing elf!" he yelled, as loudly as he could. Luckily, one of the reindeer heard his cries and stooped his head down to the snowy ground, so that Finbar could climb up his nose and antlers and hop onto Santa's shoulders.

"Why, Finbar!" gasped Santa, who was very pleased indeed to see the little elf. "Thank goodness you're all right. We've been looking everywhere for you."

"How did you know I was missing?" asked Finbar, sighing with relief.

"Well, young elf," began Santa. "When you didn't come back to work, the other elves went to look for you. They couldn't find you anywhere around the Grotto, and then I remembered that the reindeer had flown off for a practice run around the same time that you'd gone missing. I guessed that you must have flown off with them, but when you didn't return I knew something must be wrong."

Santa went on to explain that they had to wait until nightfall before they could come out looking for him. It wouldn't do for humans to see Santa's sleigh, especially

when it wasn't even Christmas Eve yet.

As soon as the world was asleep, the reindeer had set off once again to look in each of the places they had stopped the night before. Santa went with them to help. He was very worried about what might have happened to Finbar.

"I was thinking all kinds of awful things. What if you'd fallen out of the sleigh? Oh dear. We were all in a panic, I can tell you."

"I'm sorry I caused so much trouble," Finbar said softly, "but I do so love acorns."

"Well, never mind. It's a relief to get you back in one piece," Santa sighed.

The next morning, Mia and Louis set off early for the park, just as they had promised, to look in the border of bushes. There was no sign of Finbar.

"I suppose he must have gone then," said Mia thoughtfully. "I just wish we could be sure." It was then that Louis noticed some tiny little footprints in the snow, which they followed eagerly. The footprints led to some rather unusual tracks in the snow.

"I think these are sleigh tracks!" cried Louis. Then Mia suddenly noticed her doll's coat lying on the ground.

"Finbar went home," they said together, grinning at each other.

A few days later it was Christmas Eve, the most exciting night of the year. But as Mia and Louis hung their stockings up, their thoughts weren't only of presents and the treats they might get.

"Mum, can we leave out some treats for Santa?" asked Louis.

"Of course," replied Mum, "how thoughtful!"

They left out a mince pie for Santa, a carrot for the reindeer...and some acorns.

"Acorns?" Mum remarked, puzzled.

"That's right," declared Mia.

"Elves love them, you know!" added Louis, smiling to himself.

A Very Special Gift

by Gaby Goldsack

It was Christmas Eve, and Princess Rosie was very excited. She'd been saving for a long time, and now she had enough gold coins to buy her Dad, the king, an absolutely fabulous present.

"I want something that's shiny and sparkly that costs lots and lots of money," she told the man behind the counter at the royal jewellers.

"How about this?" said the man, showing Princess Rosie a gold chain.

"Not expensive enough," said Princess Rosie.

"Then how about this?" he asked, holding out a shiny silver tie pin.

"Not sparkly enough," replied

Princess Rosie.

"Well, how about this diamond ring?"

"Too small," declared Princess Rosie. "I want something much bigger and better than that to show my father just how much I love him."

As the man rummaged around desperately trying to find something suitable, Princess Rosie looked around the shop on her own. It was brimming with expensive things that sparkled and glowed. Surely there must be something her dad would like.

Suddenly, an object that was big, shiny, and very, very expensive caught her eye. It was a beautiful clock. Its face and hands were made of solid gold, and its numbers were formed from diamonds and emeralds. Princess Rosie had never seen such a fancy clock.

"I'll take that," she shouted, pointing

an excited finger at the clock. "That really is a present fit for a king."

"But that's the most expensive thing in the shop," said the man. Then he gave an embarrassed cough. "Ahem, are you sure you can afford it, Princess?"

"Of course I can," laughed Rosie. Then she poured her gold coins out onto the counter.

"Er," gulped the man, "that looks like more than enough." He counted out the coins, then went to the till and took out a teeny-tiny little bronze coin. "Your change," he added, dropping it into Princess Rosie's outstretched hand.

Princess Rosie was so pleased with the clock that she couldn't wait for it to be delivered and decided to take it home straight away. "I just know Dad's going to love it," she thought as she raced back to the palace with her precious gift clutched in her arms.

Rosie was so busy thinking about how pleased her dad would be that she had spent so much money on him, that she didn't notice the icy puddle in the snowy palace courtyard.

"Ahhh," she screamed as she skidded and spun. "Eeeee," she cried as she lost control of her feet. "Oooooh," she gasped, as she fell on her bottom and the clock landed beside her with a CRASH!

Princess Rosie scrambled to her feet and rushed over to the clock. She hoped that perhaps she'd been lucky and it had landed softly in the snow. But the opposite had happened. The glass case had shattered and the face and hands were crumpled and bent out of all recognition. Even the sparkly jewels had flown out, and lay twinkling in the snow.

"Oh, no!" cried Princess Rosie. "Dad's beautiful present is ruined, and I haven't got any gold left to buy him another one." She dug in her pocket and pulled out the tiny bronze coin that the man in the shop had given her.

"This isn't enough for a mince pie, let alone a lovely present," she groaned. Then Princess Rosie did the only thing she could think of. She sat beside the fountain and cried. She was crying so loudly that she didn't notice Jack, the stable boy, until he was standing right beside her.

"What's wrong, Princess Rosie?" asked Jack kindly.

"I bought my dad a wonderful present,

then I dropped it, and that's all that's left," sobbed Rosie. She pointed towards the shattered remains of the clock lying in the snow. "Now I've got nothing to give him for Christmas. And I really wanted to give him a special present to show him how much I love him."

"Oh, dear," said Jack, carefully picking up the broken bits of clock. "I'll tell you what. Why don't you come back to my place and I'll see if I can fix it for you."

Princess Rosie couldn't see how a stable boy thought he was going to fix the clock, but she felt she had no other choice, so she decided to go with him.

Jack led Rosie up some steps to a room above the stable. As Jack swung the door open, Rosie closed her eyes and took a deep breath. She hoped it wasn't going to be too dirty and smelly.

But when she opened her eyes, she

was pleasantly surprised. The room was as bright and neat as a pin. It was even decorated in festive strips of holly and ivy. But best of all, there was a tree in the corner covered with lovely things.

"What are all these?" asked Rosie. She went over to the tree and stroked a carved wooden horse.

"Oh, they're the Christmas presents I've made for my family," explained Jack shyly. "The horse is for my dad. He loves horses, just like me. The knitted gloves are for my mum. She always gets cold hands, especially when we make snowmen on Christmas Day. And the wooden flute and tin whistle are for

my brother and sister."

Princess Rosie was amazed. Each present was beautifully made and really thoughtful. While Jack tried to put the clock back together, he told Rosie how he had spent his evenings making the gifts.

"They might not be grand," he smiled, "but I guess you could say that each and every one of them is made with love."

As Jack said the word 'love', Princess Rosie sat bolt upright. He had given her an idea. She could make her dad a present to show him how much she loved him. She jumped to her feet and thanked Jack for trying to fix the clock.

"If you give me a few days I think I could finish fixing it," he said.

"No, don't worry," she cried. "You keep it. I've got something else planned." She was just about to leave the room when she turned around and gave Jack a hug. "You've saved my Christmas," she smiled, and she gave him a kiss on the cheek. Jack blushed from head to foot.

"But what have I done?" he asked, looking confused.

"Don't worry. You've helped solve my present problem," laughed Princess Rosie, as she raced down the steps.

Back at the palace, Princess Rosie rushed straight to a cupboard in the schoolroom. She rummaged around until she found what she was looking for – paints, a paintbrush and some crisp white paper.

Then she got to work painting a picture of herself and her dad building a snowman. They'd never actually built a snowman together – after all, it wasn't the sort of thing that kings and princesses did – but Rosie thought it would be a nice thing to show.

Rosie painted all afternoon and into the evening. By dinnertime the painting was finished, and she left it to dry while she ate. After dinner, she took the painting to the royal carpenter's workshop, and he showed her how to make a frame for it to go in. After that, Rosie just had time to wrap it up before her dad appeared and told her it was bedtime.

Rosie was very excited when she awoke the next morning. It was Christmas Day, and she couldn't wait to give her present to her dad. But before she had even jumped out of her bed, her dad came into her room.

"I'm afraid my Christmas present to you couldn't wait any longer," he laughed, as he produced a wriggling ball of fluff from behind his back.

"Oh," gasped Princess Rosie. It was a ginger kitten. She took it from her dad and hugged it to her chest.

"Thank you, thank you, thank you," she cried. "I'll call him Duke. Shall we play with him together?"

"I'm afraid I haven't got time, Rosie," said the king. "I've got all the official gifts to open before breakfast. If I start now, I might be finished in an hour or two. Hurry down when you're ready and you can watch me."

Princess Rosie quickly got dressed and rushed down to the throne room with Duke in one arm and her dad's present in the other.

Rosie's dad was surrounded by magnificent gifts. "And this one is from the Earl of Kevil," said his chief adviser, holding out an ornate clock a lot like the one that Rosie had bought him.

"Please put it with the other clocks," said the king, waving a weary hand towards a row of more jewel-encrusted clocks.

"And this is from the Queen of Inmarsh," said the chief adviser. He placed a diamond-studded music box in the king's hands.

The king glanced at the pile of expensive gifts and gave a heavy sigh. "Are there many more?" he asked.

"Just these," said the adviser, handing the king a matching crown and sceptre.

"Put them with the other crown jewels," said the king, barely looking at them. "Is that the last of the presents?" he asked hopefully.

"Er, not quite," whispered Princess Rosie. She chewed her lips nervously. If her dad was so bored by all those splendid gifts, what would he think of her silly old painting? Perhaps she wouldn't give it to him, after all.

She tried to hide the present behind

her back, but it was no use. The king had seen it.

"Have you got a present for me, Rosie?" he asked. "Come on, don't be shy."

Princess Rosie edged forwards and shyly handed her present to her dad. "It's not much. I made it myself," she whispered. Then she grabbed Duke and buried her face in his fur so she didn't have to watch her dad open the present. Silence fell over the throne room, and Rosie wished that the ground would open up and swallow her. Then, one by one, the king's advisers and the rest of the court began to clap. Rosie wondered what was going on. She peeked out from behind Duke and blinked in surprise. Her dad had a very big, very un-kinglike grin on his face.

"This is the best, most thoughtful present I've ever received," he cried. "Come here, Rosie, give your old dad a kiss."

Then he turned to his chief adviser. "Please hang this painting over my throne," he said.

"Then tell Cook that Princess Rosie and the king are going to be late for breakfast. We're going outside to build a snowman. Merry Christmas everyone!"

The Magical Sleigh Ride

by Jan Astley

Once upon a time, in a faraway land, there lived a little girl called Tansy. Tansy lived with her mum, dad, little brother Daniel, and her beloved grandma. Tansy and her family were very happy. The land where they lived was beautiful and bright. The sun always shone, it seldom rained, and it was never, ever cold.

Sometimes, when Tansy was tucked up in bed, her grandmother would tell her tales about the chilly lands in the North where she had lived as a girl. Tansy loved hearing about her grandma's homeland, and her favourite stories were the ones about snow. Tansy had never seen snow, except in storybooks or on TV.

"Sometimes, when I was a little girl, it would snow all night long and I would wake up to a crisp white world," Grandma would tell her. "When I walked on the snow, it would crunch beneath my feet and I would leave perfect footprints behind me. And it was really soft, too. I liked to pick it up and squeeze it to make snowballs. Then I would throw them at my friends. We'd have a big snowball fight! The snow didn't hurt if it hit us, but it made us wet and, if blobs of snow went down our collars or into our boots, it made us shiver."

"It must have been fun," laughed Tansy.

"It was," smiled Grandma, "but my favourite thing was when it snowed on Christmas Day. It didn't always happen, but if it did we would go outside and make a snowman as soon as we had finished opening our presents. We'd put a carrot on his face to make a nose, and we'd make his eyes from stones. I even made a snow dog once. Then we'd be called inside for Christmas dinner, and while it was being served up we'd rub our freezing hands to warm them up."

"I would love snow on Christmas Day," sighed Tansy. She imagined what it might be like, waking up to find snow falling from the sky and settling like a white blanket on the ground. She imagined putting her fingers into it to make little finger holes, or drawing her name on it like she often did in the sand on the beach.

One day, not long before Christmas, Tansy had an idea.

"Let's write a letter to Santa," she said to Daniel, "asking him if we can have snow on Christmas Day."

Daniel thought it was a brilliant idea.

So Tansy wrote a letter to Santa Claus in her best handwriting. It read:

Dear Santa,
I live in a sunny land and I have never seen snow before. My grandma says snow is so cold you can make snowballs and snowmen out of it. Can I please have some snow for Christmas? My brother would like some too.
Love from Tansy x

When Tansy had finished, she and Daniel both signed the letter and put it in an envelope. On the outside Tansy wrote:

To Santa Claus
North Pole

Grandma gave them a stamp, and then they posted it straight away.

A week before Christmas, Tansy's dad brought the Christmas tree down from the attic and the children got to work decorating it. They covered it with balls made of fluffy cotton and put a shining star on top.

Then Tansy went outside. Grandma had told her that before it snows the whole sky is covered with grey cloud. Tansy looked up hopefully. The sky was a clear blue and the sun shone bright and hot. As usual, there wasn't a cloud anywhere.

"I wonder if Santa got my letter," she whispered to herself. "Maybe he's looking at it now and getting the snow ready to bring to us on Christmas Day."

All that week Tansy kept looking at the sky, waiting for the clouds. She was sure Santa wouldn't let her down, but every day the sky stayed blue and the sun shone brightly.

On Christmas Eve the children went to bed early. Tansy found it hard to get to

sleep. She was so excited at the thought of waking up on Christmas morning and finding some snow outside that she didn't feel sleepy at all.

She wondered how Santa would bring the snow. Would he carry it in a sack the same way he carried everyone's presents? She started to worry that as he transported the snow from the North Pole the hot sun would melt it before she had a chance to see it.

Tansy lay in bed tossing and turning, thinking about snowmen and snowy footprints. Then suddenly she heard a noise. It sounded like bells tinkling in the night sky. She got up and looked out of the window. It was dark as usual, but in the moonlight, on the grass below, she could see some strange animals.

Tansy remembered seeing some like them on a Christmas card and realized they must be Santa's reindeer. They were harnessed to a brightly painted sleigh. Next to them, dressed all in red, his face almost covered by a long white beard, was Santa!

When he saw Tansy, Santa waved. "Hurry up, Tansy," he called. "We're going on a magical journey. Go and get Daniel."

Tansy woke her brother. "Come quickly," she whispered excitedly. "Santa's here, waiting!"

Tansy and Daniel quickly dressed and ran into the garden. Santa was waiting for them, with a huge smile on his face.

"Come with me," he said, holding out his hands. "I have something for you." He gave each of the children a bundle of warm clothes. "They're for later, when it starts to get really chilly," he explained.

"Where's the snow, Santa?" asked Daniel.

"I can't bring the snow to you," chuckled Santa. "It would only melt in the sun. But I wouldn't like to disappoint you, so you're going to the snow! Now, giddy-up, my trusty reindeer," he cried. "Fly as fast as you can!"

The children held on tightly as the reindeer leaped into the air, pulling the sleigh behind them. Higher and higher they climbed, until the ground was far below them. Then the sleigh straightened up, and soon they were flying along beneath the stars. The magical sleigh ride had begun...

The happy passengers looked over the side of the sleigh as Santa steered his reindeer across the night sky. They could see the whole world beneath them. They flew over forests and rivers, jagged mountaintops and sandy deserts. Sometimes all the children could see was mile upon mile of dark countryside, and then the blackness would be broken as they passed over big cities scattered with a million lights.

"Now put on your warm clothes," Santa told them. "We're nearly there."

After a few minutes the sleigh landed. The children looked around in amazement. The whole world was completely white. Hills, fields, trees and houses were all covered in what looked like powdery, white sugar. Everything sparkled like diamonds in the moonlight.

"Snow!" the children whispered in amazement.

Tansy took off one of her gloves and touched the snow with a finger. It was just as Grandma had described it. It was soft and yet crunchy, dry and yet wet, and it was very, very cold, like an ice cube.

A door opened in a house nearby and the children saw a smiling woman standing in the doorway.

"Welcome to the North Pole, children," she smiled. "I'm Mrs Claus."

For the next few hours the children had a wonderful time. Santa introduced them to his helpers and showed them the workshop where the toys were made.

Then came the best part of all... playing in the snow.

First they made trails of footprints. Next they had a snowball fight, and it was such fun they didn't mind when little bits of snow slipped down their collars and made them shiver.

Then, of course, they made a snowman. They used two of Santa's spare black buttons for eyes and a carrot from the store of reindeer food to make his nose. Tansy wrapped her new scarf around his neck and Daniel put his woolly hat on his head. Then everybody held hands and danced around him, singing a song:

"I'm a jolly snowman round
and neat.
I've got no hands and got no feet.
I like the cold but not the heat.
Seeing you is such a treat!"

They danced and sang until they could dance no more. Then they went inside the house and warmed themselves by the fire. Mrs Claus gave them mugs of hot chocolate milk and some cookies straight from the oven. Soon they began to feel warm again. In fact the children were so comfortable that their eyes started to close, and soon they were fast asleep.

When Tansy awoke it was morning. She was no longer in the North Pole. She was in her own bed, in her own bedroom. The curtains were open and the sun was shining, but there was no snow outside. Everything looked the same as usual.

Tansy remembered her night-time adventure. Had it all been a dream? It had felt so real: meeting Santa, the journey in the sleigh and dancing around the snowman. She could even remember the song they had sung.

Feeling a bit confused, she quickly got dressed and went downstairs.

"Merry Christmas, Tansy," Grandma said, handing her a small package. It was round and hard and was wrapped in snowflake-covered paper. On a little label it said: *"To Tansy. Love, Santa x."*

Tansy opened the present carefully. Inside was a beautiful glass ball filled with snow – it was a snow-globe. In the globe there were two children and three elves dancing around a snowman. Tansy looked at it closely and her heart gave a leap. The two children looked just like her and Daniel, wearing exactly the clothes that Santa had leant them. So it hadn't been a dream, after all!

Tansy shook the globe and it began to play a familiar tune. "It's our snowman song," laughed Tansy. "And that's us, dancing around the snowman, just like we

did last night."

Tansy's parents and Grandma stared at the globe in amazement. "How did you get in there?" asked Dad.

"You'd have to ask Santa that. But I do know he gave us what we asked for," laughed Tansy. "Snow on Christmas Day!"

The Rainbow Snowman

by Kath Jewitt

Joshua opened the curtains one morning. "Hooray! It snowed!" he cried. His sister Olivia rushed to the bedroom window.

"Wow!" she exclaimed. "It's really deep! Let's go to the park and build a snowman."

The two children got dressed as quickly as they could and rushed downstairs.

"Can we take this old orange hat and the striped scarf with holes in it for our snowman, Mum?" asked Olivia.

Mum smiled. "Of course," she said. "You can have my old red skiing gloves, too. They're worn out, but they'll do for a snowman, I think."

All the way to the park Olivia and Joshua made footprint trails through the snow. When they arrived they were thrilled to find that nobody else had been to the park yet, and the snow looked perfectly smooth. They ran around, making circles, squares and zigzag lines of footprints as if they were scribbling on a clean white page.

"Let's build our snowman now," suggested Joshua. "We could do it right next to the Christmas tree by the bandstand."

"Yes!" agreed Olivia. "Then he can join in the carol concert tonight. If we dress him up in the bright clothes Mum gave us, everyone will notice him."

The two children got to work. Using their feet, they scooped up a big mound of fresh snow. Next they piled armfuls of snow on top, patting it down with their gloved hands, until the mound was almost up to Joshua's shoulders.

"Now for the head," panted Olivia. She squeezed together a snowball and rolled it down a slope. Over and over it tumbled, gathering snow as it went. Bigger and bigger it grew, until Olivia and Joshua had to push it on their hands and knees.

"It MUST be big enough now," puffed Olivia, brushing the snow off her wet knees. "We won't be able to lift it if it grows any more."

Together, the two children hoisted the giant snowball into the air.

PLONK! They placed it firmly on top of the snow mound.

Now the snowman had a lovely fat body and a big round head. All he needed were some finishing touches. Olivia went hunting for two long spiky sticks and then she stuck them either side of the snowman's body to make his arms. Joshua made his face with pebbles and a carrot he had put in his pocket earlier, knowing that all the best snowmen have a carrot for a noise. Finally, they dressed their snowman in the bright-orange hat, red gloves and the long, multi-coloured scarf that their mum had given them.

"He looks great," laughed Olivia. "He must be the most colourful snowman in town – and I think he knows it! It looks like he's smiling."

Soon other children came to play in the park, and they all admired the jolly snowman. His smile made them feel happy. He seemed to be encouraging them to enjoy the lovely crunchy snow.

Eventually the town clock struck twelve. "Lunchtime!" cried Joshua, patting his rumbling tummy. "I thought I was feeling hungry."

"Me too," agreed his sister. "It's hard work making snowmen. Let's go home. I need to warm up a bit."

Olivia and Joshua waved their snowman goodbye. "See you later," they shouted. "We'll be back for the carol concert tonight."

It was cold in the park, and it was getting colder all the time. As the afternoon went on, the sun dipped lower and lower in the sky. Soon the snowy ground began to freeze. The park emptied until finally the snowman was left all alone, with just the shivering park animals for company.

"I hope our snowman is all right," said Joshua worriedly, as he and Olivia sat at home, all cosy and warm. "It's freezing out there, you know."

"He'll be fine," said Mum. "Snowmen don't mind the cold. Anyway, he's got all those colourful old clothes to keep him warm, hasn't he."

But that was where their mum was wrong. It's true that snowmen don't mind the cold. After all, they are made of snow. But Joshua and Olivia's snowman didn't have an orange hat any more, or a striped scarf, or even a pair of red gloves. All his clothes were gone.

The orange hat was now a cosy nest for the shivering birds. The worn-out red

gloves had become beds for a family of mice...And the long, multi-coloured scarf with holes in it? It made a perfect lining for the rabbits' burrow in the frozen ground.

That evening, when Joshua and Olivia arrived at the park for the carol concert, they wriggled their way to the front of the crowd.

"Mum! Dad! Come and see our colourful snowman," they pointed. But of course, the snowman wasn't colourful any more. He was as plain and white as any ordinary snowman.

"Oh," cried Olivia and Joshua in disappointment. "Where are his clothes? No one will notice him now."

Just then, the crowd fell silent. The mayor had arrived to turn on the Christmas tree lights and start the carol concert.

"THREE, TWO, ONE. MERRY CHRISTMAS!" roared the mayor, as

he flicked the switch. In an instant, the Christmas tree lit up like magic, casting coloured light over the snow.

"Wow!" cried Olivia and Joshua in unison. "Look at our snowman."

The light from the Christmas tree was making the snowman glow lots of different colours, just like a rainbow.

"Oooh!" gasped the crowd. "Look at the rainbow snowman. Isn't he amazing? And look at that smile. He must be the happiest snowman in town."

And, do you know, he WAS.

Leave It to Rudolph

by Jan Astley

It was Christmas Eve at the North Pole, and it was snowing hard. Santa and Mrs Claus were rushing around loading bulging sacks of presents onto the sleigh. It was their busiest night of the year, and they were running late.

"Hurry, hurry," urged Mrs Claus. "It's time for you to leave!"

"Just one more sack to go," answered Santa, huffing and puffing as he staggered toward the sleigh. But the ground was icy. Santa slipped and fell, landing with a crash in the snow.

"Ouch!" he cried. "I think I've twisted my ankle."

Mrs Claus helped Santa back inside and found a bag of frozen peas to put on his swollen ankle.

"The cold will make it feel a little better," she explained.

Rudolph the reindeer shook his head sadly. It didn't look as if Santa would be going anywhere in a hurry tonight. His ankle had puffed up like a balloon. He couldn't walk, much less climb up and down chimneys.

"What are we going to do?" wailed Mrs Claus. "Tomorrow is Christmas Day, and children everywhere must have their presents!"

"You'll have to go instead of me," sighed Santa, clutching his sore ankle.

"But I don't know where all the children live," replied Mrs. Claus.

"Leave it to Rudolph," Santa reassured her. "He's my cleverest reindeer. He'll know what to do."

When Rudolph heard the plan he

shook his head again. His memory wasn't as good as Santa thought it was. He wasn't sure he *could* remember where all the children in the world lived, even if he was a magical reindeer. But he didn't want to panic Mrs. Claus, and Mrs. Claus didn't want to disappoint the children, so she kissed Santa goodbye and climbed into the sleigh.

"I'll give it a go," thought Rudolph to himself. "I'll probably remember where everyone lives eventually."

Sure enough, things went well at first. The journey went pretty well, and Rudolph did manage to remember where everyone lived. He was able to show Mrs Claus where to go to deliver the presents to the right children.

But then they reached Melford, the very last town on their route.

"Now, Rudolph," said Mrs Claus.

"The first present I have to deliver here is a sparkly ballet dress for Sarah Smith. Do you know which house is hers?"

Rudolph looked around, feeling puzzled. His nightmare had come true. He had forgotten where anyone lived in Melford! What was he going to do?

Rudolph had to guess. Otherwise they'd be in Melford for hours, and eventually people would wake up and see them. That would be a disaster, and he would be the one to blame.

Rudolph swallowed hard and pointed a hoof towards a red door in a row of houses.

"Twenty-three Oldgrove Street?" asked Mrs Claus.

Rudolph nodded, hoping for the best.

From then on, things seemed to go smoothly. Rudolph helped Mrs Claus deliver a giant fluffy toy rabbit to Tom

Bennett at 24 Oldgrove Street, and a shiny red bike to Katie Brown at number 25.

Last of all, Mrs Claus squeezed down the tiny chimney at 6 Walnut Lane to deliver a pair of silver and blue soccer boots to Ashley Jones. She even managed not to wake up the puppy that was asleep at the foot of the bed.

At last all the present sacks on the sleigh were empty.

"Well done, Rudolph! We've finished for another year. I rather enjoyed doing Santa's job, but no wonder he comes home so tired every Christmas morning. There are so many chimneys to climb up and down in the world."

"And so many addresses to remember," Rudolph thought. He was very glad to be going home. They headed back to the North Pole, and Mrs Claus was feeling very pleased with herself.

When they got home, Mrs Claus went into the house to see Santa. His ankle was much better. "How did it go?" he asked.

"Rudolph remembered everything, even the children in the last town of all, Melford," said Mrs Claus proudly.

"Sarah at 23 Oldgrove Street got the ballet dress she asked for, and Tom at number 24 got his rabbit. We delivered the bike Katie wanted to number 25, and Ashley's soccer boots went to 6 Walnut Lane. Everything went very well."

As Santa listened carefully to what his wife was saying, his eyes grew wider and wider. Then he got up and pulled on his long, black boots.

"Wake up the reindeer," he called. "We're going out again."

"What?" cried Mrs Claus? "We've delivered all the presents!"

"Yes, but we have to go back to

Melford," explained Santa. "Sarah Smith doesn't live at number 23 – that's where Ashley Jones lives. Sarah lives at 6 Walnut Lane. And Tom doesn't live at number

24 – that's Katie Brown's house."

Mrs Claus looked horrified.

"Are you saying that everybody got the wrong presents?" she stuttered.

"That's exactly what I'm saying,"

nodded Santa sadly. "We've got more work to do before dawn."

Rudolph felt terrible when he heard the news. Santa said it couldn't be helped, and it could have happened to anyone, but Rudolph hated the idea that he would be responsible for disappointing the children of Melford on Christmas morning.

When Santa and the reindeer got back to Melford, they could hear a rooster crowing – it was Christmas morning! At any moment the sleigh might be spotted by somebody when they opened their curtains and looked out. There wasn't a single minute to lose.

Santa shot in and out of chimneys as fast as he could, putting everything right. Luckily, with the help of the bag of peas, his ankle had made a full recovery.

He quickly grabbed the toy rabbit from the end of Tom's bed and rushed over to

Katie's house with it. He grabbed the shiny red bike from Katie's house and crept back to Tom's house with it.

Then Santa squeezed down the tiny chimney at 6 Walnut Lane and found the soccer boots that were meant for Ashley.

Sarah's puppy was at the foot of the bed, but he didn't stir. Santa wriggled back up the chimney and carried on sorting out the whole messy mix-up as fast as he could.

All that was left to deliver was the ballet dress to Sarah at 6 Walnut Lane. Santa squashed himself into the chimney one more time and placed Sarah's present on her bed next to the sleeping puppy.

"I'm not going back up that tiny chimney again," he thought. "I'm running out of time. I'll use the back door instead." But just as he was creeping out, Sarah's puppy ran into the back yard, barking loudly. He wanted to play with the funny reindeer and ride on the sleigh!

"Ssssh," cried Santa. "You'll wake up the whole town." But the puppy didn't understand, and barked even louder.

"This time you CAN leave it to me," smiled Rudolph. He could speak animal language, which is something that Santa didn't know how to do.

He lowered his head until he was touching noses with the noisy puppy. Then he said something in animal language to the puppy, who understood him perfectly.

"Woof, woof, woof," replied the puppy, and he trotted back inside, wagging his tail.

"Good job, Rudolph!" said Santa. "You may have been a bit forgetful earlier, but you've saved Christmas after all. Now let's go home, for good this time!"

With one last weary effort, the reindeer leaped into the air. And by the time all the children woke up on Christmas day, Santa, the reindeer and the sleigh had completely disappeared. They were all back at the North Pole with Mrs Claus… fast asleep!